Fun with Fingerprints

by Natalie Lunis

Table of Contents

What Are Fingerprints?

Look at the skin at the tips of your fingers. Can you see lots of little lines that curve and swirl? Do the lines make a **pattern**?

Use a **magnifying glass** to look closely at one fingertip. How does the pattern look now?

pattern

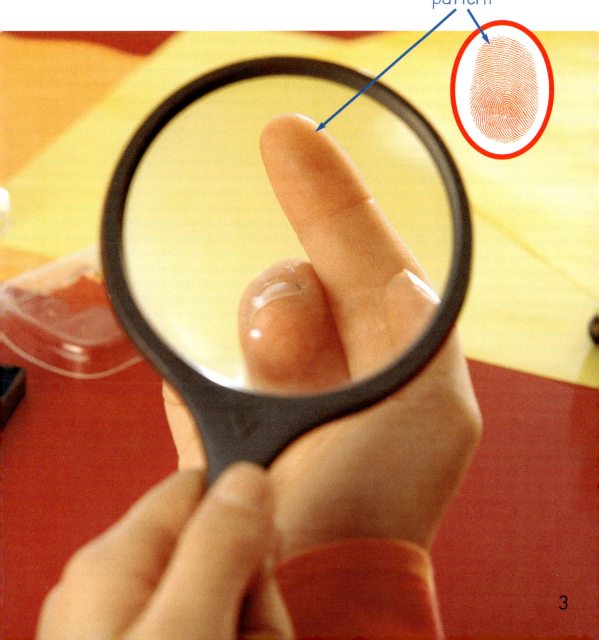

The patterns that you see are called **fingerprints**. Every person has his or her own fingerprints. No one else has fingerprints that look just like yours.

Do you know that **twins** often look exactly alike? But even twins who look alike have different fingerprints.

How Can You Make a Fingerprint on Paper?

You can follow these steps to put your fingerprint on paper. Keep trying until you get a nice, clear print. And wash your hands when you are finished!

Here are the things you will need:

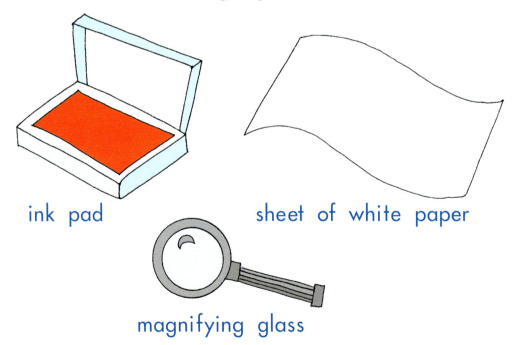

ink pad

sheet of white paper

magnifying glass

Step 1 First, choose one fingertip and press it on the ink pad.

Step 2 Now press your fingertip on the paper.

Step 3 Now lift your finger.
Look at your fingerprint.

Step 4 Use the magnifying glass
to look at the print up close.
Can you see the pattern?

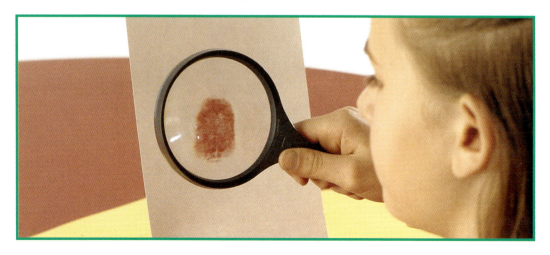

How Can You Make a Set of Fingerprints?

Here's how to make a set of prints for all five fingers.

Here are the things you will need:

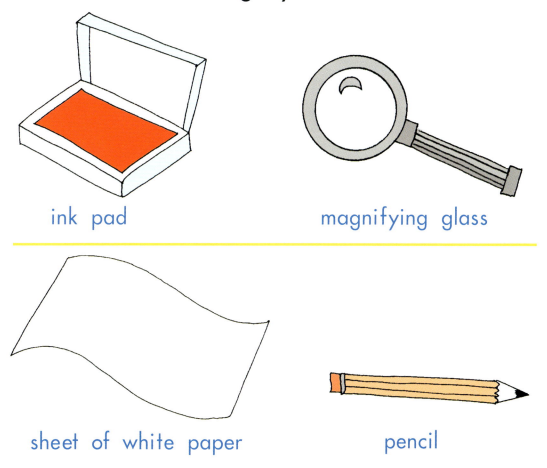

ink pad

magnifying glass

sheet of white paper

pencil

Step 1 You should place the sheet of paper sideways. Now draw five boxes.

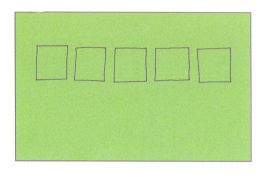

Step 2 Look at this picture of a child's right hand. It shows the name of each finger.

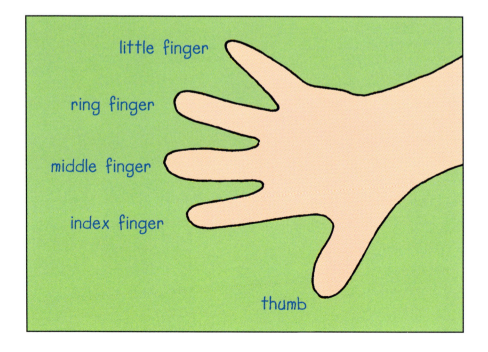

little finger

ring finger

middle finger

index finger

thumb

Step 3 Write "Right Hand" above the five boxes. Then write the names of the fingers under the boxes.

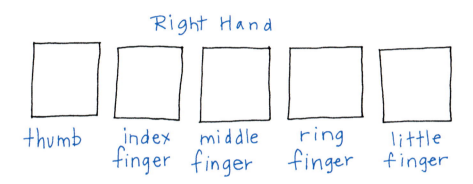

Right Hand

thumb   index finger   middle finger   ring finger   little finger

Step 4 Press your right thumb on the ink pad and make a print in the box you marked for the thumb. Do the same for the other fingers of your right hand.

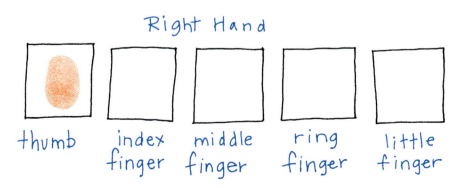

Right Hand

thumb   index finger   middle finger   ring finger   little finger

11

Step 5 Now look at your paper. You have made a full set of fingerprints.

Right Hand

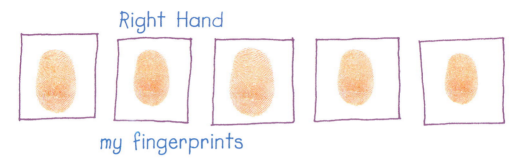

my fingerprints

Step 6 Show a friend how to make a set of five fingerprints. Look at your friend's prints. Then look at your own. Do the prints look different?

Right Hand

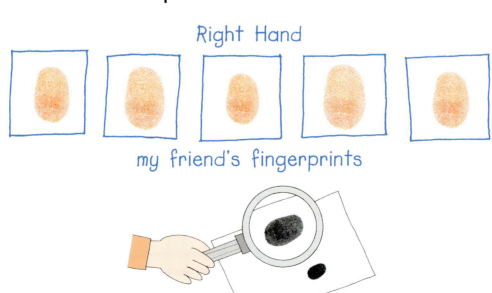

my friend's fingerprints

How Can You Make Fingerprint Art?

You can use fingerprints to make fun pictures. Try the ideas on these pages. Then try your own ideas.

Here are the things you will need:

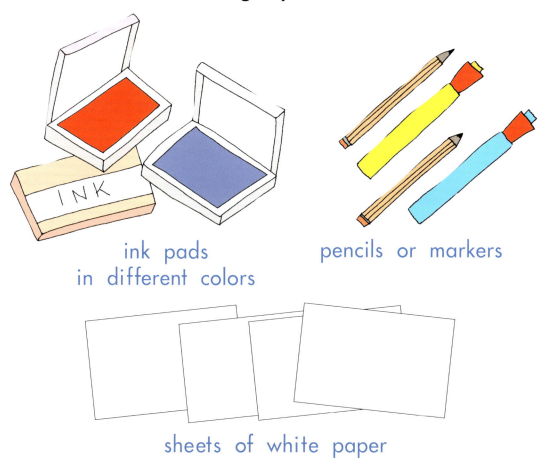

ink pads
in different colors

pencils or markers

sheets of white paper

Step 1 Make a few fingerprints on the sheet of paper. Use different fingers and different colors.

Step 2 Now use the fingerprints to make little animals. Add eyes, ears, noses, legs, and tails.

dog   bird   pig   fish

Then make a big picture full of fingerprint shapes.

Glossary

fingerprints (FIN-ger-prints): the pattern of tiny lines on the skin of your fingertips

magnifying glass (MAG-nih-fy-ing GLAS): a piece of glass or plastic that makes things look bigger

pattern (PA-tern): something that repeats over and over

twins (TWINZ): two brothers, two sisters, or a brother and sister who are born together

Index